A STUDENT'S GUIDE TO
PHILOSOPHY

ISI GUIDES TO THE MAJOR DISCIPLINES

GENERAL EDITOR   EDITOR

JEFFREY O. NELSON   JEREMY BEER

A STUDENT'S GUIDE TO PHILOSOPHY
BY RALPH M. MCINERNY

A STUDENT'S GUIDE TO LITERATURE
BY R. V. YOUNG

A STUDENT'S GUIDE TO THE STUDY OF HISTORY
BY JOHN LUKACS

A STUDENT'S GUIDE TO POLITICAL PHILOSOPHY
BY HARVEY C. MANSFIELD

A STUDENT'S GUIDE TO ECONOMICS
BY PAUL HEYNE

A STUDENT'S GUIDE TO LIBERAL LEARNING
BY JAMES V. SCHALL

A STUDENT'S GUIDE TO THE CORE CURRICULUM
BY MARK C. HENRIE

A STUDENT'S GUIDE TO U.S. HISTORY
BY WILFRED M. MCCLAY

A STUDENT'S GUIDE TO PSYCHOLOGY
BY DANIEL N. ROBINSON

A STUDENT'S GUIDE TO CLASSICS
BY BRUCE S. THORNTON

A STUDENT'S GUIDE TO AMERICAN POLITICAL THOUGHT
BY GEORGE W. CAREY

A Student's Guide to Philosophy

RALPH M. MCINERNY

WITH A BIBLIOGRAPHICAL APPENDIX
BY JOSHUA P. HOCHSCHILD

ISI BOOKS
WILMINGTON, DELAWARE

Cataloging-in-Publication Data

McInerny, Ralph M.
      A student's guide to philosophy / by Ralph
   McInerny. —Wilmington, Del. : ISI Books, 1999.

         p. cm. (ISI Guides to the Major Disciplines)

         ISBN 1-882926-39-0
         1. Philosophy. 2. Philosophy—History.
   I. Title. II. Series.

B75.M35   1999   99-66785
190—dc21   CIP

Published in the United States by:

   ISI Books
   Intercollegiate Studies Institute
   Post Office Box 4431
   Wilmington, DE 19807-0431

            Cover and interior design by Sam Torode

         Manufactured in the United States of America

CONTENTS

AN INTRODUCTORY NOTE

❧

"TO ASK WHETHER OR NOT one should philosophize is already to philosophize." When Aristotle said that he might have meant that doing philosophy is something like speaking prose—although you have been doing it all along, it still comes as news to be told that you are. Inevitable though it may be, philosophy has had a long and checkered career since its beginnings in the sixth century B.C. How a philosopher regards that history can tell you a lot about what kind of philosopher he is.

Modernity begins with the assumption that philosophy has yet to begin. Descartes first doubts everything he has been told. No judgment can cease to be suspect until it has passed a number of methodological tests that he devises. It is not sufficiently emphasized that this means that no one can claim to know anything until he has subjected it to methodic doubt. If methodic doubt begins with Descartes, as he claims, then philosophy had no pre-Cartesian history. Or its history is simply a record of error and deception.

Since Descartes, philosophers have vied with one another to seek an originality that would distinguish them from the rest of the pack. The drive for originality usually entails a very negative attitude toward one's predecessors, and the history of philosophy inevitably loses its interest. When I was a graduate student I was urged to read Hans Reichenbach's *The Rise of Scientific Philosophy.* For Reichenbach, philosophy began with Immanuel Kant in the eighteenth century since all pre-Kantian philosophy involved a fundamental mistake. More recently, we have been told that moral philosophy is based on a mistake and, in 1903, G. E. Moore showed to his own satisfaction that all previous moral philosophy was fallacious. In the 1930s A. J. Ayer looked back a few years to when philosophy had really begun. Later still, a linguistic turn was taken and, we were assured, philosophy could now at last get started.

From this and my opening remark, you can conclude that a sure sign that one is doing philosophy is to claim that it has never been done before. There is a tradition of denying tradition, in other words. There are inventive ways of handling previous attempts, however. Heidegger undertakes a destruction of the history of ontology in order to work his way back to the point where things first went wrong. This suggests that, while the past of philosophy was brief, it did occur.

In the Nietzschean phase we have now reached, philosophers are urged to forget about truth and become "strong poets." The remark suggests an odd conception of poetry and an even odder one of philosophy. The implication is that poets simply emote and philosophers should follow suit. Leszek Kolakowski has written that "A modern philosopher who has never experienced the feeling of being a charlatan is such a shallow mind that his work is probably not worth reading." You will of course wonder how Kolakowski was feeling when he wrote that. Perhaps in the tradition of such remarks—I think of the Liar's Paradox—the speaker is implicitly exempted.

There is a more cheerful estimate of the history of philosophy that is captured by the phrase "perennial philosophy." This is meant to suggest that, beneath and beyond the wrangles and differences and diversity of philosophies, there is a subtle progress being made such that every philosopher contributes *malgré lui* to a cumulative achievement of the race.

These few introductory remarks indicate the circumstances in which one sets about writing a student's guide to philosophy at the end of the second millennium. Philosophy has come to see itself as winding down, reaching the end of its rope on a gallows of its own construction. One might attempt a *wertfrei* account of the terrain, giving a narrative of what philosophers are doing here and there, staying above the battle, and accepting the by now mandatory disdain for philosophy's past. That is not how I intend to proceed.

What follows will be an effort to direct the beginner to the great sources of philosophy as to fonts of truth. Newman said of Aristotle that he had expressed our thoughts before we were born. And of course Dante called Aristotle the master of those who know. Accordingly, this guide will concentrate on Aristotle and the later developments of his thought. I share Pope John Paul II's dismay, expressed in *Fides et Ratio* (Faith and

Reason), that philosophers seem wary of the big questions, the questions that in a sense define us. What does it all mean? Does life have a purpose? Is death the end? Is there a God? This little guide will give directions on where philosophical help can be found to address such questions as these.

THE PURSUIT OF WISDOM

THERE IS A THEORY about the dialogues of Plato—at least some of them, the "Socratic" ones—that their function was to stir up interest in potential members of the Academy so that they would want to devote their lives to the pursuit of philosophy. Literary recruiting posters, as it were. The Greek adjective here is "protreptic." The idea is that there is a desire that precedes and guides the pursuit of wisdom.

In his phlegmatic way, Aristotle put it thus: "All men by nature desire to know." To be a human being is to have a built-in natural thirst for knowledge. A bent is natural if we have it whether or not we choose to. We become aware that it is already at work in us. Now this can seem a rather exalted thing to say about everyone. You might have an acquaintance or two, perhaps a relative, of whom it would seem outlandish to say that he has a natural desire to know. He might seem to have a natural desire not to know. Was Aristotle carried away by his intellectualistic and Macedonian tendencies? Not at all. He goes on to say this about our natural desire to know: "A sign of this is the pleasure we take in our senses. . . ." The general claim is verified in this modest and convincing way. Sensing is something we are engaged in without taking thought, so it is natural in the sense required, and it is by and large pleasant to sense, particularly to see, to take a look: "[F]or even apart from their usefulness they [the senses] are loved for themselves; and above all the sense of sight. For not only with a view to action, but even when we are not going to do anything, we prefer seeing (one might say) to everything else. The reason is that this, most of all the senses, makes us know and brings to light many differences between things."

We find already adumbrated in this account of sensation the distinction between the practical and theo-

retical. Our senses are instrumental—we call them or-
gans, after all—and their most obvious role is in helping
us live our lives. We look out. We are on the lookout.
The outlook is favorable or not. But surely Aristotle is
right that just looking is sometimes its own reward. For
all that, the pleasures of sense are dangerous if they become an end in themselves, but that is only because the
human good embraces and transcends them. Experience
retains (i.e., records) the history of perception and may
give way to art. The experienced person has know-how,
but it is the mark of the artisan that he knows both
How and Why. When it is a question of the specifically
human, *Why* marks the spot.

SOCRATES (469–399 B.C.), an Athenian war veteran, loved to
discuss philosophical topics in the marketplace. He wrote nothing
and is known to us only indirectly—in a play of Aristophanes, in
Xenophon, and, most importantly, as the hauntingly wise inter-
locutor of many dialogues of Plato. The *Crito* and *Apology* provide
us with moving portraits of a comrade "who was, we may fairly say,
of all those whom we knew in our time, the bravest and also the
wisest and most upright man" (*Phaedo*, 118). The *Apology* professes
to be Socrates' reply to the judges who have falsely accused him of
corrupting the young. It ends thus: "Now it is time that we were
going, I to die and you to live, but which of us has the happier
prospect is unknown to anyone but God" (42).

When Plato observed that philosophy begins in wonder, he was thinking of two senses of wonder—the wonder that is awe and the wonder that comes from not yet knowing why. The Athenian who witnessed a solar eclipse two and a half millennia ago felt much the same awe we do. His understanding of what was happening may strike us as risible, but a true explanation does not take away our wonder. The wondering involves the wonderer as well. What does it all mean? And what does it mean for me to be in this world?

We are these questions, in a sense, and the pursuit of them, often latent in everyday activities, sometimes absorbing us completely, draws us through and beyond the world to the source of ourselves and all the rest. From its beginning, theology was the ultimate business of philosophy. When Plato said that philosophy is learning how to die he was not being morbid. It is the inescapable fact of our mortality that provides the horizon for our thinking.

"All men by nature desire to know." This truth is a great leveler; it leaves no one out. It prevents us from thinking that some are thinkers and the rest are, well, the rest, the many, the *hoi polloi*. Everyone is already engaged, well or badly, in thinking and in that sense is already a philosopher. Potentially, as Aristotle would add. Latently. But the capacity is there in every human. The questions are inescapable. Perhaps we have to learn not to philosophize, making a real effort to put our minds to leading mindless lives. If being dumb is the achievement, one is not likely to preen himself on being a philosopher.

If I seem to protest too much this is because of the gall of Descartes. How could he induce us to doubt everything when all along we have to remember how to

---

PLATO (427–347 B.C.), an Athenian aristocrat whose thought pointed in the direction of active political involvement, spent much of his life, at home and abroad, seeking to bring the practical into line with the ideal. Athens was conquered by Sparta and put under the control of the Thirty Tyrants, among them relatives of Plato. The restored democracy condemned Socrates, whose student Plato had been. Plato departed for southern Italy. There were Pythagoreans there and, in Syracuse, the tyrant Dion. When Plato returned to Athens in 387, he founded a school, the Academy. Several times he returned to Syracuse, in the hope of making Dion into a "philosophical king," but with disappointing results. The last thing Plato wrote was the *Laws,* far less known than the earlier *Republic,* but the fruit of bitter experience. Twenty-six dialogues of Plato have been preserved, in many of which Socrates is featured. Plato remains the most accessible of philosophers, at least in his early works, and his influence is only rivaled by that of Aristotle.

read French or Latin? What the return to Aristotle gains us is the realization that everybody already knows things for sure. Of course the observation is banal, but that is only one of its attractions. It is also true. Philosophy starts where everybody already is. The principles of philosophy are in the public domain. The modern tendency is to say, "Hang on to the brush, I'm taking away the ladder." With Arisototle, we will keep our feet firmly on the ground.

GETTING THERE
⤜

IF WISDOM IS THE GOAL and the definition of wisdom is "such knowledge as men can achieve of the divine," how do we get from here to there? The middle books of Plato's *Republic* lay out a curriculum for the aspiring philosopher. Once the appetite has been whetted, once the desire for knowledge is deep, the student is ready for some sobering news. He must devote a decade to the study of mathematics. Paideia is a structured process. We do not begin just anywhere.

From Aristotle we can piece together the proper

order of learning the philosophical sciences and the reason for it. We begin with logic, so we will recognize good arguments when we meet them; we go next to mathematics, because even children can learn it. Not much experience of the world is needed to do arithmetic and geometry. Then on to natural philosophy, which will occupy us for years and years. The world is a given but nature delivers up her secrets only to the persistent

---

ARISTOTLE (384–322 B.C.), a Macedonian whose father was physician to Alexander the Great, allegedly a pupil of Aristotle's. He came to Athens, where he spent nearly two decades in Plato's Academy, until the death of the master. Then, perhaps disappointed at not being named head of the school, Aristotle founded his own, the Lyceum. The chief Platonic teaching, that only ideal entities separate from sensible things are really real, was much debated within the Academy; but Aristotle devised an alternative to it. With him philosophy became systematic and his works, derived from his lecture notes, put us in contact with the one Dante called "the master of those who know." The range of Aristotle's interests— logic, natural science, ethics, politics, aesthetics, metaphysics, rhetoric, statistics of Olympic winners—gave shape to the human desire for knowledge, dividing inquiries into different sciences. The Aristotelian treatises, apparently lost, were edited in more or less their final shape by Andronicus of Rhodes in the first century. Since then, in the original or in translation, they have exercised an indelible influence on Christian and Islamic culture and to this day remain the preferred reading of philosophers.

inquirer. Experience of another kind, of good and evil, is required if the study of moral and political philosophy is to be profitable. The young see things in black and white while the favorite adverb of the aged is "perhaps." Truth in the moral order makes itself known to the virtuous. Finally, we are ready to ask if there is any science beyond all these (i.e., the science of being as being). That culminating effort comes to be called metaphysics.

The fragments of this pedagogy that became the monastic education of the Dark Ages were called the liberal arts tradition. On the one hand, there was sacred learning, the Bible, and on the other, secular learning, the

---

AUGUSTINE, SAINT (354–430), was born in the town of Thagaste in what is now Algeria and spent the end of his long life as bishop of Hippo in the same province. His tumultuous early life prior to his conversion to Christianity is told in the *Confessions*. The most important of the Latin Fathers of the Church, Augustine battled the Pelagian and Arian heresies. His massive *City of God* contains, in Book Eight, a sketch of the history of philosophy as Augustine understood it. Perhaps the most influential post-apostolic figure in Christendom, Augustine is claimed by Protestants and Catholics alike and serves as a bridge between them. Augustine translated the Platonic Ideas into the creative Ideas in the Divine Mind, that is, the Logos, the second person of the Trinity. This modified Platonism continues to appeal.

seven liberal arts. The *trivium* consisted of grammar, rhetoric, and logic; the *quadrivium*, of arithmetic, geometry, astronomy, and music. It was as if the whole of human learning, the fragments that had been shored against our ruin after the collapse of the classical world, could be gathered into those arts. Desirable as these arts were, they were also aimed beyond themselves—*trivium,* the threefold way, *quadrivium,* the fourfold way. Ways to what? To the wisdom contained in the Word of God.

Universities arose in the thirteenth century from the monastic and cathedral schools and, with the arrival of Aristotle, the liberal arts were restored to the larger context they knew in Plato and Aristotle. They were now seen as only parts of secular learning, not the whole of it. We can see that the *trivium* and *quadrivium* answer to the first two stages in the order of learning in the philosophical sciences mentioned earlier. From its beginning, medieval education sought to establish a *modus vivendi* between faith and reason. This remained true in the thirteenth century. The recovery of philosophy had to be accommodated to the theology based on Scripture. For one brief shining century everything cohered.

The last great effort of idealism is phenomenology. The return "to the things themselves" disappointingly became a concern with the constituting acts whereby objects become objects (i.e., the conditions of presence), and what had seemed a realism became one more effort to tease from the structure of our mind the character of its objects, to anticipate experience, to turn thinking into a kind of thing-ing that generates its own object. This alteration of the program of phenomenology caused the recently canonized Edith Stein to part company with Edmund Husserl.

Phenomenology, like drugs, is addictive. Imagine

BOETHIUS, ANICIUS MANLIUS SEVERINUS (480–524), Christian writer and Roman citizen, held various political posts in Rome and worked with Theodoric, the Ostrogothic emperor. Boethius set out to translate into Latin all of Plato and Aristotle and then show their fundamental agreement. This superhuman project had achieved only translations of some Aristotelian logical works before he stopped work on it. As a Catholic, Boethius entered into the theological debates of his time. He published a number of theological tractates (e.g., *On the Trinity*). Accused by Theodoric of conspiring against him, Boethius was condemned to death. Awaiting execution in Pavia, he wrote the five books of *The Consolation of Philosophy,* in each of which prose and poetry alternate. After the Bible, it was the most copied book in the Middle Ages. The Aristotelian works Boethius translated played a crucial role in medieval education.

finding sentences like the following meaningful: "In fact, after Nietzsche had brought to an end and completed all the possibilities—even inverted—of metaphysics, phenomenology, more than any other theoretical initiative, undertook a new beginning" (Jean-Luc Marion). It would be more accurate to say that philosophy, both Continental and analytic, succumbed to Teutonic gurus

---

AQUINAS, THOMAS (1225–1274), born at Roccasecca, was sent at the age of five to the great Benedictine abbey at Montecassino, which was in the neighborhood. From there, as a teenager, Thomas went to the University of Naples to continue his studies. There he met members of the new Dominican Order and joined, to the consternation of his family, who had imagined him entering Montecassino and ending up as abbot. Thomas studied with Albert the Great in Cologne and completed his theological studies at the University of Paris. From 1265–1268, he taught at Paris and then returned to various Dominican houses of study in Italy. He came back to Paris in 1268 and taught there until 1272. He was assigned to Naples and died while on his way to the Council of Lyon in 1274. The arrival of vast amounts of Aristotle in Latin translation fractured the relation between faith and reason that had characterized early medieval education. It was Thomas's achievement to welcome Aristotle and to show that his thought is compatible with Christian faith. His *Summa Theologiae*, unfinished, is his most important theological work. Apart from various philosophical treatises, Thomas commented on a dozen of Aristotle's works. In Thomas all previous strands of thought were woven into a synthesis.

who uttered gnomic pronunciamentos. The influence of a Heidegger and a Wittgenstein can be difficult to comprehend, yet these are the two most influential philosophers of our century. Each proclaimed himself to be a new beginning. Ezra Pound, in his *Cantos*, sought to produce lines like the uneven ones in the remnants of Sappho's verse. Some modern philosophers aspired to write pre-Socratic fragments. The style was aphoristic, arguments were scarce to nonexistent, a mood was induced or an attitude produced which ruled out questioning. Nietzsche was tolerable because the madness had no method. In Heidegger, Nietzsche is given credit for having brought metaphysics to an end, whatever that might mean. Heidegger is the first post-metaphysical thinker. He must be; he tells us so. Wittgenstein sought to redefine philosophy, yet boasted in old age that he was a professor of philosophy who had never read Aristotle. One would have bet on it.

There is little sign that the influence of Heideggerian and Wittgensteinian gnosticism is abating. Like a fever, it will have to work itself out. Meanwhile, academic philosophy is in the doldrums, light-years distant from the questions that alone can justify it. If one could make sense of the claim that all—all!—the possibilities, inverted or not, of metaphysics had been brought to an end and completed by mad Nietzsche, one might agree or disagree. But what would either mean? It is best to heed Jeeves's remark to Bertie Wooster. "You would not like Nietzsche, sir. He is fundamentally unsound."

It may seem a relief to turn to analytic philosophy from the polysyllabic breathlessness of Continental phi-

---

DESCARTES, RENÉ (1596–1650), is known as the father of modern philosophy. Schooled by the Jesuits, roughly in the Scholastic tradition, Descartes entered the army and one night experienced a series of dreams which inspired his intention to put philosophy at last on a solid foundation. His *Discourse on the Method* and *Meditations*, the reading of which must make every pulse race, reenact for the reader the process he went through. Testing every idea and thought by asking if it was possible to doubt it, Descartes eventually exhausted the inventory of his mind. At this dark point in the drama, it occurred to him that even if he were always deceived in thinking he knew something, he could not be deceived about the fact that he who was deceived exists. From this starting point, he went on to prove the existence of God and then, on the basis of God's veracity, the existence of the external world. He spent his relatively short life in study, answering objections, writing letters. He was in Stockholm as the guest of Queen Christina when he died. Among his papers was found a memo on which he had recorded the dreams which had been at the origin of his intellectual career.

losophy. But this is to turn from Heidegger to Wittgenstein, the one as enigmatic as the other. The linguistic turn, like the transcendental turn, aims at putting philosophy in any traditional sense out of business. The seemingly straightforward desire to establish the meaning of meaning has not met with success. So we are back at the beginning; philosophy in the twentieth century, like philosophy in the sixteenth, is still trying to get started. Its present state is obscure, its past nonexistent, and its future nothing worth waiting for.

To say that modern philosophy has abandoned classical and medieval philosophy is simply to accept its self-description. Since this has still not led to anything, perhaps it is time to question the wisdom of the abandonment.

It is not just a well-turned phrase that modern philosophy is the Reformation carried on by other means. Most of the major figures are Protestant or apostate or both. Luther's attack on reason and his Manichean split between nature and grace poisoned the well of thinking. There is a striking contrast between the popular view that, thanks to science, our knowledge of the world increases by quantum jumps, and the philosophy of science, which robs the achievement of realistic import. Is it the world we know or our knowing of the world? Can't we always substitute one paradigm for another? Unmoored in sound philosophy, science becomes technology and the sorcerer's apprentice is let loose.

Since modern philosophy is characterized by the rejection of the past, I intend to return the favor and proceed for the nonce as if modern philosophy had not happened. Only after we have proceeded on this basis will we return to modern and more recent philosophy. Skepticism about the recent past of philosophy is almost *de rigueur* now, so it will be important to ask whether the iconoclasm of the past several paragraphs is merely received opinion.

NEWTON, ISAAC (1642–1727), is one of two or three towering figures in modern science. He taught at Cambridge, was a member of the Royal Society, discovered the law of gravity, and wrote (in Latin) his *Mathematical Principles of Natural Philosophy*. Newtonian physics explains things in terms of motion and quantitative and measurable data. Both original and incorporating the discoveries of Galileo and Descartes, Newtonian physics reigned supreme until Einstein.

COMMON SENSE?

WE HAVE CONTRASTED modern philosophy with classical by saying that, while the former seeks an absolute starting point for thought, the latter notices that we have been thinking all along and asks what our starting points were. The modern mode could be shown to be a begging of the question, but the classical would seem to be committed to taking seriously the general opinions of mankind. Is this an appeal to common sense? Why not? Well, think of all the oddities that have been commonly held. In the immortal words of William Tecumseh Sherman, "Vox populi, vox humbug!"

There is a kind of school of philosophy called Common Sense, most notable in its Scottish form. This school is said to hold that we should simply begin with the fixed beliefs of mankind and go on from there. After all, there is no way to escape these, and to what else can appeal be made to correct them if the appeal must commend itself to human thinkers? Rather than discuss this in the abstract, let us examine Aristotle's procedure when, in setting out to study physical objects, that is, things that have come to be as a result of a change and are constantly changing (i.e., natural things), he puts before us a bewildering array of views as to what nature is.

Aristotle holds that there are common starting points for human thinking, principles that no one can fail to know. And yet, as he emphasizes, his predecessors have held views on the source of change whose variety boggles the mind. How can there be such diversity and conflict on matters which lie right before the eyes? Anyone who reads the first book of Aristotle's *Physics* will notice the respect with which Aristotle recounts views which are on the face of it absurd. Along the way, he provides extenuating reasons, particularly for post-Parmenidean accounts. Parmenides (b.515? B.C.) taught that the world of change and multiplicity had to be illusory because it violates the most elementary rules of logic. If change occurs, he held, being and non-being are the same. The atomists, Anaxagoras, and others sought to give an account of the changing world which softened the suggestion that any real change was occurring. But it is what Aristotle does after describing the rival views of his predecessors that interests me now.

He is concerned to ask what, despite all their differences, these views have in common. Some said that nature was water and others said that it was fire or air; some spoke of elements, others of atoms, some of the infinity of parts of an infinity of kinds of things as constitutive of any macrocosmic body. Bedlam? Babel? Or are there latent agreements beneath the obvious differences? Aristotle suggests that all these accounts share the notion that change involves a subject and contrary states

---

HUME, DAVID (1711–1776), historian, diplomat, and philosopher, was born in Edinburgh. In 1734, he moved to La Flèche in France (where Descartes had been educated) and began his *Treatise of Human Nature*. He expected fame and glory from the three-volume work, but it was greeted with resounding silence. His *Moral and Political Essays*, published in 1742, enjoyed success but not enough to gain him a chair at the Unviersity of Edinburgh. He became secretary to a general and traveled in Europe, but an appointment as librarian in 1752 enabled him to return to Edinburgh and write his *History of Great Britain*. In Paris in 1763 he moved in *philosophe* circles. When he broke with Rousseau, he returned home. Among his late works is *Dialogues Concerning Natural Religion*. Almost offhandedly Hume criticized the tendency to conclude from a series of observations—sentences featuring Is—that one Ought to do something. This split between is and ought—sometimes called Hume's guillotine—has had a long and fateful history.

of the subject. This analysis suggests that, while an initial appeal to the opinions of mankind is going to produce a seemingly unmanageable diversity, a closer look will detect beneath the diversity a common recognition. It is these deep, or shallow, perhaps, agreements that Aristotle has in mind when he talks about common-starting-points. And this is a community that can be drowned out by the middle distance noise of diversity.

KANT, IMMANUEL (1724–1804), was born and lived and died in Königsberg, where he became professor of philosophy and was legendary for the clockwork regularity of his lifestyle. Kant wrote much before the famous "critical turn," but it is the Kant of the various *Critiques—of Pure Reason, of Practical Reason, of Judgment*—that looms as one of the handful of giants in the history of philosophy. A rigorous examination of our means of knowing reveals that our sensibility and reason provide a priori forms which, when imposed on the sensible manifold, generate the phenomena with which sciences treat. Metaphysics, according to Kant, is the effort to apply a priori forms where they do not apply: our concepts can never range beyond the realm of the stuff which is a necessary component of any object of thought. This means that God and other immaterial things, the objects of metaphysical quest, cannot be thought. Proofs of God's existence are all invalid since they involve an illicit move from what we can know to what, according to Kant, we can't. Kant found room for God in the practical order, where he is most famous for the categorical imperative, a rule of moral judgment. Unless we can will that the content of our moral judgment be universally valid for all actions, we are not acting morally.

Does Aristotle think that, just because all previous accounts of natural change have implicitly invoked three principles, that it is thereby established that there are three principles of change? Not quite. All he concludes from this is the *likelihood* that this is true. The likelihood is grounded on the realization that all these people, like ourselves, have minds and standard cognitive equipment.

PLATO OR ARISTOTLE?

Ϡ

EARLIER WE SPOKE of the proper order of learning that can be gleaned from Aristotle and mentioned that, if we sought in Plato an account of the process of learning, we would be drawn to the vivid story told in the middle books of the *Republic*. Socrates tells us to imagine prisoners in a cave, chained so that their eyes are fixed on the back wall. Behind them, halfway to the entrance, there is a ledge that screens off a fire. Slaves walk behind that ledge holding up figurines whose shadows are cast on the back wall of the cave. The prisoners take the shadows to be real and their talking and thinking bears on them. Unchain these prisoners and turn them gently around. The light of the fire nearly blinds them, but eventually their eyes become used to it and they see the figures. Their epistemological allegiance is switched from the shadows to the images. The story continues with the prisoners gradually being led out of the cave, into the light of the sun, where they see the really real.

This is one of the most memorable passages in philosophical literature and it is a crime to substitute this poor precis for it. The first state of the prisoners is not one of

---

NEWMAN, JOHN HENRY (1801–1890), Oxford don and Anglican priest, was involved in the Oxford Movement, which sought to locate the English church midway between Protestantism and Catholicism. Members of the movement became interested in the Fathers of the Church and such episodes in Church history as the Arian heresy. In a series called *Tracts for the Times*, the Oxford Movement put its case to the English people. Eventually, as he recounts in *Apologia Pro Vita Sua*, Newman argued himself into the Catholic Church. This made him a pariah to many and he resigned his Oxford fellowship, withdrawing to Littlemore, just outside the town. His life as a Catholic was a cultural and social comedown. Old Catholics were wary of him and his former Anglican brethren shunned him. As a Catholic priest, Newman lived in a community in Birmingham, continuing to write. His *Essay in Aid of a Grammar of Assent* was written over many years. *The Idea of a University*, lectures delivered in Ireland when he was rector of the Catholic university there, is Newman at his most accessible. He was made a cardinal by Leo XIII in 1879.

diversity so much as unanimity in deception. Aristotle, on the other hand, gives us a picture of superficial diversity and latent unanimity. These are differences and there are others between Plato and Aristotle, but one fundamental common assumption is that everyone has a capacity to know. Is it possible that the prisoners, any more than Aristotle's predecessors, should be 100 percent wrong?

CONFUSED CERTAINTIES

IT WAS NOT BY ACCIDENT that I turned to the *Physics* for a discussion of the relationship between first principles and common sense. At the outset of that work, Aristotle observes that the process of learning moves from a first confused though certain knowledge and progresses to ever more distinct knowledge of the particular things we sense. These particular things are grasped by the mind via general notions and the claim is that we begin with the most general intellectual grasp of them and then seek to achieve ever less general and more specific knowledge. We see something afar off and are sure that there is something there, but what? It moved; it is coming toward us;

it seems to be moving itself rather than blown along by the wind. Is it an animal? Why, it seems human; look at those arms; look at those legs, and that face. Good grief, it's my mother-in-law. So it is that we get progressively more precise fixes on things. Our intellectual knowledge begins with the most universal.

No wonder Aristotle looked for common, shared, more universal recognitions latent in the views of his predecessors. However implicit such recognitions are, they are there to be drawn out. When drawn out and made explicit, they are revealed to be the common starting-points of human thought. Aristotle goes on to argue that it is indeed the case that every change involves three factors: a subject and contrary states of that subject. The product of any change can be described as a complex of the subject and a new state, of matter and form. He then turns to Parmenides, but tells us that in doing so he is adopting a viewpoint which is more comprehensive than that of natural philosophy. The defense of the reality of change is not a task of the natural philosopher, but of the metaphysician, to whom is assigned the defense of first principles.

SOPHISTRY CONFRONTED

ॐ

THE VERY FIRST PRINCIPLE of reasoning is the so-called principle of contradiction. It receives various expressions. [1] "It is impossible to affirm and deny the same predicate of the same subject simultaneously." [2] "It is impossible for a proposition to be true and false at the same time." [3] "It is impossible for a thing to be and not to be at the same time and in the same respect." These variant expressions are not without their significance for the question of the relationship between first

---

NIETZSCHE, FRIEDRICH (1844–1900), brilliant son of a Lutheran minister, had felt a youthful attraction to the cloth, but turned to classical philosophy instead. He was diverted from a brilliant academic career by the music of Richard Wagner, against whom he violently turned. It is impossible to characterize the writings of Nietzsche—they are unique in their style, flair, and iconoclasm. One of his characters, a madman, declares that God is dead and we have killed him. Nietzsche announces a post-Christian era where all the supports of theism have been removed. With God goes nature and any basis for maintaining the truth or falsity of judgments. Dostoyevsky's nihilist had said that if God does not exist, anything is permitted. Nietzsche seems to have held that out of the ashes and rubble of Christendom something new and better would arise. He ended his life in madness.

principles and common sense.

An obvious response to [1] is to say, "But of course I can." What could be easier than saying, "I am six feet tall and I am not six feet tall"? And I mean at the same time and in the same sense of the predicate. How can this be impossible if it is so obviously possible? The impossibility lies in the statement's being intelligible. The proposed counterexample does not succeed in asserting a contradiction; it fails to be an assertion. Expression [2] may be called the epistemological version of [1], but both of them ultimately repose on [3], the ontological statement. What we say and what we think are ultimately grounded in the way things are–and of course speaking and thinking are themselves instances of being. Socrates cannot be in the room and out of the room at the same time–not in the same sense. Arguing children ultimately fall back on this same truth. "It is." "It isn't." "It is." "It isn't." Whatever "it" is in the dispute, the disputants are as one in knowing that it either is or it is not.

Plato and Aristotle saw sophistry, the dark twin of philosophy, as the subversive effort to undermine first principles. In responding to Sophists, Plato may seem to be more shocked by their moral deficiencies, while Aristotle rather concentrates on the fallaciousness of their reasoning. The attack on starting-points poses a tough methodological question. If these are indeed the starting-points, first principles, to what can appeal be made in their defense? If arguing is normally drawing out the implications of prior truths and there are no truths prior to first principles, we seem to be naked to our enemies, without resources against those who, like the Sophists, assert their opposites.

One can argue for first principles, but obliquely. One takes the opponent's claim as good money and then

---

HEGEL, GEORG WILHELM FRIEDRICH (1770–1831), brought German philosophy to an apotheosis in absolute idealism. In many ways a philosopher's philosopher, Hegel operated at a distance from ordinary discourse and language. His *Phenomenology of Spirit* (a.k.a., *Phenomenology of Mind*) is typical in its range and obscurity. The work deals successively with consciousness, self-consciousness, reason, spirit, religion, and absolute knowledge. Hegel's system was meant to subsume everything into itself and is in many ways a Christian philosophy. He famously held that philosophy is the truth of religion, thereby stirring Kierkegaard into indignant rejection of Hegelianism. The route to God is not so much nature as history, and Hegel felt that the philosopher could discern the necessity in the temporal flow.

shows that it cannot be cashed; it is counterfeit. In short, one employs the *reductio ad absurdum*, displaying the incoherence of the claim. Let me single out what is Aristotle's ultimate example of such a *reductio*. One who denies the first principle will either state his denial or not. If not, there is nothing to discuss. If he states it, he will say something like, "It is possible for a thing to be and not to be at the same time and same respect." The corresponding contradictory remarks are simultaneously true. The language in which one says this employs words; words have meanings. If his words have meaning, that is, mean what they mean and not something else, then the denial invokes the principle it purports to reject. If

---

HUSSERL, EDMUND (1859–1938), began as a mathematician and made his reputation with two volumes of *Logical Investigations*. Dismayed by the seemingly endless quarrels between philosophical systems, Husserl urged concentration on the data to be explained rather than rival explanations. The phenomelogical method was intended to provide as accurate and faithful an account as possible of the given, of what appears, of the data. "To the things themselves!" was the slogan, and many rallied around Husserl, finding in his method a renewal of realism. But with *Ideas*, Husserl took a fateful turn, focusing on the a priori conditions of phenomena, thereby losing the allegiance of Edith Stein, his assistant, and many others.

on the other hand, the denial applies to the denial, then it ceases to be a denial but is equally an affirmation.

The delight that one might take in such refutations is minimal and in any case a fleeting thing. At the end, one has only acknowledged the beginning. It is not nothing to have swept from the field one who questions whether there is a field, but the mind seeks meatier sustenance. For all that, it is a continuing task to address those who would engage in philosophizing only to subvert it.

PHILOSOPHY IN AN AGE OF SCIENCE

IT IS OFTEN SAID that twentieth-century philosophy is defined in terms of its interest in language. The linguistic turn followed on the epistemological turn and the suggestion was that language was the source of philosophical problems. But these problems are due to misunderstanding and must be addressed by a therapy aimed at showing that they should never have arisen in the first place. The aim of philosophy is to put philosophy out of business. Unfortunately, this seems to be an endless business. On the Continent it was held that Greek and German are the only philosophical languages and that they are the House of Being. Heidegger is its shepherd, making him, as Harry Redner has wittily pointed out, the German Shepherd of Being. But surely it is the rise of the sciences that characterizes modernity.

Nietzsche lamented that modern man, having acknowledged the death of God and the folly of Christianity, transferred his allegiance to science and made of the scientist a kind of priest. There are certainly those who, dismissing all pre-Copernican efforts, would tie the possibility of knowledge exclusively to the sciences. What is the status of philosophy vis-à-vis the sciences? One might of course simply identify the two, or, as a variation on this, describe philosophy as a reflection on the procedures and attainments of the scientist. But what are we to make of the fact that, during the very centuries when science gained its ascendancy, the most influential philosophers were questioning the ability of the human mind to know the world? Enamored of Newton and chastened by Hume, Kant despaired of knowing things as they are, what he called "noumena"; insofar as we do know things we know them as we know them—that is, as spatio-temporal, as causing and caused, and the like. But these are categories of our sensibility or of our understanding which, while they organize our experience, cannot be taken to be an account of how things are in themselves. How are things in themselves? By definition, we can never know.

Pure Reason bears on the a priori conditions of sensibility and understanding, the epistemological cookie-cutters that shape our experience. And where is the world of action? Kant allows that somehow in acting we are involved in the real world; but that can scarcely provide the measure of what we ought to do. Kant notoriously provides the most abstract rule of action, the categorical

---

RUSSELL, BERTRAND (1872–1970), was an English aristocrat, Cambridge philosopher, and co-author with Whitehead of the *Principia Mathematica*, a landmark in modern formal logic. Russell's personal life was colorful—he embraced atheism and pacificism, and wore himself out in old age in efforts to condemn the United States. Over his long career, his views evolved and changed. An enthusiast about Wittgenstein, whose work he thought close to his own philosophy of logical atomism, Russell became dismayed with his protégé.

imperative. This is the Kantian version of the fact/value split, to which we will turn in a moment.

Can it be the case that all prescientific knowledge must be swept away and must cede its place to a scientific account? The question can be understood either with reference to the past or as a present issue. Have all previous—at least pre-Copernican—statements about the natural world been confined to the dustbin of history? It is helpful to transpose the question to the present. What is the status of my knowledge of the world that antedates, accompanies, and survives scientific explanation? It will not do to say that all non-scientific knowledge must be

---

MOORE, GEORGE EDWARD (1873–1958), taught at Cambridge, where he was the friend of Bertrand Russell, Alfred North Whitehead and, eventually, Ludwig Wittgenstein. There is an engaging clarity in Moore's writings. His abiding passion was to rid British philosophy of the influence of Absolute idealism, hence his famous defense of common sense. His most influential work was the *Principia Ethica* (1903), which had an off-campus impact on the Bloomsbury group, Lytton Strachey, and Virginia Woolf, et al. Moore held that moral philosophers were wrong to try to define the good in terms of any physical or empirical characteristics to things called good. Goodness was a non-natural property directly intuited. This led to the "naturalistic fallacy," which cut morals loose from any definable connection with the empirical.

discarded. For one thing, it provides a necessary point of reference to scientific explanation. Everyday physical objects are solid; they weigh in the hand; they have a taste; and they cool or warm the hand that holds them. Color, taste, smell—aren't these the secondary qualities which are replaced by a quantitative account of them? But consider the claim: Quantitative accounts are accounts of things attained in ordinary experience. If the color I see is illusory, there is nothing to explain, only something to explain away. This does not do away with the scientific revolution, of course. But our description of what happened may be less exuberant. If we have come to prefer quantitative accounts of qualitative experiences because they are more amenable to manipulation and to gaining control over our environment, then, that is what happened. But this does not show that the original experience was illusory.

This leaves open the question as to the value of accounts and analyses of this so-called prescientific experience. Obviously, much philosophical analysis is a version of this, and whatever value it has can scarcely be stated in "scientific" terms. Furthermore, such fundamental analysis as that already referred to at the beginning of the *Physics* has not been ruled out of court by methodological fiat. The analysis of change into three components—subject and contrary states of the subject—and of the product of change—a subject under a description—when taken on their own terms, as the first and most general things that one can say about physical objects, are as good now as they ever were. And what of the analyses of place and time and motion offered by Aristotle? Have they really all been swept away?

It is not nostalgia that prompts such questions. Un-

HEIDEGGER, MARTIN (1889–1976), German philosopher, colleague of Edmund Husserl, was born a Catholic, studied to become a Jesuit, but left the seminary to pursue an academic career. For career reasons, Heidegger repudiated the faith of his fathers, adopting the Lutheranism of his wife. This betrayal was echoed in his affiliation with the Nazi party before and during his rectorship at the University of Freiburg. His thought is a gnostic variation on Kant, which seeks in human subjectivity the a priori conditions of thinking. His major work, *Being and Time,* remained unfinished. Heidegger's thought became progressively more obscure and incantatory. Holding that philosophy had reached an impasse, he sought the point where it had gone wrong by setting out to systematically destroy the history of ontology. The original sin was to divorce the subject and object, man and world. Heidegger was a mesmerizing lecturer and his written work continues to impress otherwise strong minds.

less such analyses as those Aristotle undertakes in his natural philosophy and those undertaken today by philosophers who are certainly not doing science can be appraised by criteria other than those of science, science itself becomes unmoored and ceases to be a human enterprise.

THE FACT/VALUE SPLIT
❧

MODERN MORAL PHILOSOPHY defines itself in terms of the unbridgeable difference between facts and values, between Is and Ought. When G. E. Moore defined the "naturalistic fallacy" in his *Principia Ethica* of 1903, he made canonical the import of a skeptical question of David Hume and the practice of Kant. When we evaluate something (i.e., call an action good), there is nothing in what the action is that accounts for its having this value. A gap is opened up between descriptive and evaluative statements that can never be closed. The belief that a more thorough and careful description of a situation will reveal why it must be called good or bad is fallacious. Moore thought we just intuit goodness the way we do yellow, but could offer us no help when intuitions differ.

The slogan became: Anything whatsoever can be called good. Nature neither justifies nor prevents a positive evaluation. Value terms express our subjective reaction to the objective and are unanchored in it.

Alasdair MacIntyre has written that what began as one meta-ethical theory among others eventually swept the field. We are all emotivists now. Universal Emotivism, he called it, meaning that moral disagreements have universally come to be regarded as conflicting subjective reactions to states of affairs. Since such conflicts cannot be adjudicated by objective appeals, various dark possibilities loom.

This is of course untenable. Such an account of human action amounts to a denial that there are objective starting points for human action. Moral principles are as arbitrary as any application of them. This has to be addressed in the way that sophistic attacks on first principles are addressed. The position must be seen to be incoherent. A convenient way of seeing this is by considering the infamous Kennedy Decision. U.S. Supreme Court Associate Justice Anthony Kennedy, in an opinion rejecting restrictions on abortion, opined that it is a fundamental human right to be able to define existence, human life, and the universe itself as one wishes. Of such a statement one may say: If it is true, it is false. If I have such a fundamental right, I can employ it to define Justice Kennedy, his decision, and indeed the Supreme Court out of the universe. The Kennedy decision is not simply false. It is literal nonsense. And it can be taken as an adequate stand-in for Universal Emotivism.

STEIN, EDITH (1891–1942), student of Husserl and eventually his assistant and collaborator, was born into a Jewish family, lost her faith at the university, but in 1921, as the result of reading St. Teresa of Avila's autobiography, became a Catholic. Unable to secure a university teaching post because she was both a woman and of Jewish ancestry, taught for a decade in a teacher's college. She had published her dissertation, *On the Problem of Empathy*, and had written a comparison of Husserl and Thomas Aquinas. As a Catholic, she translated works of Thomas Aquinas and Cardinal Newman. It was not until it became illegal for Jews to teach anywhere that she fulfilled her deep desire to become a Carmelite nun in 1933, entering the convent in Cologne. By 1938, she feared her presence there endangered the other nuns, and she was transferred to a Carmelite convent in Holland, at Echt. On July 26, 1942, the Dutch bishops protested the Nazi treatment of Jews. Edith was snatched from her convent and put on a train to Auschwitz, where she was exterminated. She was canonized as a saint by Pope John Paul II in 1998. *On Finite and Eternal Being*, her most important philosophical work, was published posthumously.

Like Gibbon looking out over the ruins of imperial Rome, we can survey the moonscape of modern philosophy and find in it a powerful incentive to devote our time to the reading of Plato and Aristotle and the classical philosophy that was so cavalierly dismissed by the father of modern philosophy.

PHILOSOPHY AND RELIGION
ૐ

IN ITS CLASSICAL ORIGINS, philosophy was theistic. In the Christian era, there was a succession of attempts to establish a *modus vivendi* between philosophical inquiry and religious belief. The liberal arts tradition, which characterized medieval education from Augustine to Aquinas, sought to summarize the whole of secular learning into seven liberal arts, divided into two groups. The arts of the *trivium* (grammar, rhetoric, and logic) and the arts of the *quadrivium* (arithmetic, geometry, astronomy, and music) were ways because they were considered to be preparatory to the study of Sacred Scripture. Cassiodorus Senator, who lived a century after Augustine and was a contemporary of Boethius, gave this a definitive statement in his *Institutiones*. With the recovery of Greek philosophy and the introduction of Arabic science in Latin translation beginning in the late twelfth century, the matter of faith and reason had to be rethought, since reason was now seen to have a far greater reach than the liberal arts tradition had realized. During the thirteenth century, most notably in Thomas Aquinas, a new synthesis was achieved. But this began to unravel almost as soon as it had been achieved, and by the fourteenth century the reach of reason had been consider-

---

WITTGENSTEIN, LUDWIG (1889–1951), was an Austrian who studied aeronautical engineering at the University of Manchester. After three years he moved to Cambridge to study the philosophy of mathematics under the tutelage of Bertrand Russell. His early education had been scientific and technical, and he was attracted by efforts to mathematize logic. He served in the Austrian army during World War I and published in 1922 his only book, *Tractatus Logico-philosophicus*. While this seemed to be a variation on Russell's *Philosophy of Logical Atomism*, it was not reductionist in intent. Its message was that anything that can be said is relatively unimportant; the truly important escapes the net of language. Wittgenstein had association with the Vienna circle but taught at Cambridge where he became a legendary and enigmatic figure. A shelf full of his works have appeared posthumously, edited by devoted students, the most important of which is *Philosophical Investigations,* which rescinded the conclusion of the *Tractatus.*

ably diminished. Nominalists questioned our ability to grasp the natures of things since they doubted there were natures to be grasped; the existence of God and the immortality of the soul, truths which Aquinas considered capable of being established by natural reason, were now said to be tenable only on the basis of the faith, because they had been authoritatively revealed. With the Protestant Reformation came the idea that for centuries the Christian message had been distorted by Rome and that the solution was for every believer to become his own pope, consult the Scriptures, and attend to the Spirit in grasping their truth. The dissolution of Christendom was underway.

When Nietzsche's madman comes into the marketplace crying that he is looking for God, he becomes an object of derision. The scoffers have not yet recognized that God is dead, but they have killed him. With Nietzsche begins the post-Christian age, which can be defined as the time when it is assumed that there is no God and that religion can be accounted for in psychological or economic terms. In any case, the search for truth no longer has any positive interest in theism; furthermore, it must be seen as in a polemical relation to Christianity. This is where we more or less are today.

WHY I AM A THOMIST
᠙

IN 1879 POPE LEO XIII issued an encyclical called *Aeterni Patris,* which inaugurated the revival of the study of Saint Thomas Aquinas. Leo looked out over the modern world and did not see the sunny prospect many of his contemporaries saw. Indeed, the pope found influential views of man and nature and human society to be severely flawed. It is one thing to appraise the modern world with the eyes of faith; it is another thing to do so with the common principles of human thought, that is, philosophically. It was a philosophical revival that Leo hoped for, and as its paladin, he pointed to Thomas Aquinas.

It is because, as a philosopher, Thomas found his principal inspiration in Aristotle that he can serve the function Leo envisaged for him. The foregoing sketch has doubtless revealed my conviction that philosophy must enter the third millennium on an Aristotelian note.

But this must be properly understood. It must not be understood as the suggestion that, while there is a plurality of viable philosophies, we ought to choose Aristotle. If that were the case, the choice would be arbitrary. If it is not the case, it is because there is no radical plurality of viable philosophies. Differences among philosophers are only radical when one of them is wrong. Where there is truth there is compatibility.

Thomas, we are sometimes reminded, was not a Thomist. Indeed he was not. Nor was Aristotle an Aristotelian. Both denials are correct because what the two engaged in was not a *kind* of philosophy. They simply did philosophy. Philosophy is what proceeds from principles which guide all human thinking. It is because we live in a time when these very starting-points have been called into question that the first order of business is to defend the range of reason. Perhaps it is no accident that it is John Paul II, in his encyclical *Fides et Ratio* (Faith and Reason) who urges philosophers to regain the sense of the power and scope of human reason. The believer cannot view his faith as elevated on the rubble left by modern philosophy. If one accepts truths beyond the capacity of human reason to comprehend, as one does by the gift of faith, there is needed a contrast with truths which are grasped by human reason and within the reach of all. In that sense, faith needs philosophy.

Philosophy is the lingua franca of believers and non-believers alike. It has fallen on evil days. But the seeds of its renewal are present in every human mind, in the starting-points which can only be denied at the price of incoherence. Aristotle said it, but it was true before he said it and it is still true today. "All men by nature desire to know."

APPENDIX:
A BIBLIOGRAPHICAL ESSAY
BY JOSHUA P. HOCHSCHILD

ॐ

THERE ARE SEVERAL VOLUMES which can complement the present guide as introductions to philosophy: Jacques Maritain, *An Introduction to Philosophy* (New York, 1935); J. M. Bochenski, *Philosophy: An Introduction* (Dordrecht, 1962); and Pierre Hadot, *Philosophy as a Way of Life: Spiritual Exercises from Socrates to Foucault* (Oxford, 1995). Mortimer J. Adler has spent a lifetime introducing people to the world of ideas; some of his many volumes that can helpfully orient a beginning student are: *The Conditions of Philosophy: Its Checkered Past, Its Present Disorder, and its Future Promise* (New York, 1965) and *The Four Dimensions of Philosophy: Metaphysical, Moral, Objective, Categorical* (New York, 1993). Josef Pieper's classic, *Leisure, the Basis of Culture* (New York, 1952), cannot be recommended too highly as a portrayal of the classical understanding of philosophy.

Despite these worthy books, it must be emphasized that the beginning student should spend his time becoming familiar with primary rather than secondary texts, with classics rather than with books about classics. The works put out in paperback by such publishers as Hackett, Penguin (Penguin Classics), and Oxford (World's Classics) can still be taken as a good indication of the texts regarded as most important in the history of philosophy.

This bibliography will proceed to identify some of the most important of these texts, but it will also indicate secondary sources which will help the beginning student to understand and appreciate them. New students of philosophy should not hesitate to turn to general reference works for the kind of background that normally would be supplied in undergraduate introductory philosophy courses. Some courses, and the present guide itself, presume a fair amount of literacy in the history of philosophy. For orientation with respect to the general teachings of, influences on, and significance of particular philosophers and texts, some obvious sources are the eight volumes of the *Encyclopedia of Philosophy*, edited by Paul Edwards (New York, 1967) and the ten volumes of the *Routledge Encyclopedia of Philosophy*, edited by Edward Craig (London, 1998). Also very valuable as a reference work for intellectual history is *The Catholic Encyclopedia* (New York, 1917). The online *Stanford Encyclopedia of Philosophy* (http:// plato.stanford.edu).

❧

SOCRATES (469–399 B.C.) is considered the father of philosophy, but he left no written works. That leaves **Plato** (427–347 B.C.) and **Aristotle** (384–322 B.C.) as indisputably the most important ancient philosophers to read, and their works are available in numerous translations. Plato's dialogues are by far the best place to begin reading philosophy. Besides individual works put out in paperback by the publishers mentioned above, students will find it useful and economical to acquire single-volume collections; most of Plato's writings are compiled in *Plato, The Collected Dialogues*, edited by Edith Hamilton and Huntington Cairns (Princeton,

NJ, 1961), a volume unrivalled until the recent publication of Plato's *Complete Works*, edited by John M. Cooper (Indianapolis, 1997). Of Plato's dialogues, *Euthyphro* is a good place to start, giving a sense of the dialogue form and the Socratic style, but a fuller sense of the Socratic and Platonic understanding of philosophy is gained from *Apology*, *Phaedo*, and *Gorgias*. (It can also be illuminating to compare Plato's portrayal of Socrates with that by the Greek comic playwright Aristophanes in *The Clouds* and with Xenophon's "*Apology*" or "*Trial of Socrates*.") *Meno*, *Symposium*, *Theaetetus*, and *Phaedrus* are also rewarding dialogues for new students of philosophy. Of course nobody should go very long without reading and rereading Plato's *Republic*; the famous cave allegory mentioned in this guide is in Book VII.

While it is fairly easy to get a grasp of Plato's writings, Aristotle's texts are more difficult—less literary, more systematic, and highly technical. Students may find it helpful to turn to an introduction to Aristotle's thought, either in a general history of philosophy (some will be listed below), or in the form of independent volumes; Henry B. Veatch's, *Aristotle: A Contemporary*

Appreciation (Bloomington, IN, 1974) is an excellent guide, and Mortimer Adler's *Aristotle for Everybody: Difficult Thought Made Easy* (New York, 1978) is a rare and effective attempt to introduce Aristotle to beginners. Students may also find it useful to turn to A. E. Taylor's, *Aristotle* (New York, 1955) or W. D. Ross's *Aristotle* (London, 1923; third edition, 1937).

Nonetheless, students should not rely for their understanding of Aristotle on these or other secondary works and should proceed as early as possible to reading Aristotle directly. A useful collection of Aristotle's writings, still in print and also often available at a reasonable price in used bookstores, is *The Basic Works of Aristotle*, edited by Richard McKeon (New York, 1941). While a classical education would have started with his logical works (*Categories, On Interpretation, Prior and Posterior Analytics, Topics*), most modern students will find it preferable to begin with *Physics* and *Nicomachean Ethics*, and then *De Anima* ("On the Soul"), all texts which undergraduate students should be expected to know. In addition, the beginning of the *Metaphysics* contains valuable reflections on the nature of philosophy and Aristotle's views of his predecessors; Aristotle's discussion of the principle of contradiction is found in Book IV, chs. 3 and 4 of the *Metaphyiscs*.

Students should aspire to read more of the *Metaphysics*, but it is a notoriously difficult book. Unfortunately most modern scholarship on the text is not very illuminating. The best twentieth century works in English are Giovanni Reale, *The Concept of First Philosophy and the Unity of the Metaphysics of Aristotle* (translated by John R. Catan, Albany, 1980), and Joseph Owens, *The Doctrine of Being in the Aristotelian Metaphysics* (Toronto, 1951; third edition, 1978). For a thorough, line by line treatment, students should not hesitate to turn to the indispensable thirteenth century commentary by Thomas Aquinas, translated by John P. Rowan as *Commentary on Aristotle's Metaphysics* (1961, revised edition 1995).

To understand both Plato and Aristotle it helps to have some knowledge of their predecessors, the so-called **pre-Socratic philosophers**. For primary texts the best place to turn is G. S. Kirk and J. E. Raven, *The Presocratic Philosophers* (Cambridge 1957; second edition, with Malcolm Schofield, 1983).

For philosophical writings from the period of philosophy which immediately followed Plato and Aristotle, a good selection of primary texts can be found in *Hellenistic Philosophy: Introductory Readings*, translated by Brad Inwood and L. P. Gerson (Indianapolis, 1988); a more complete collection of texts is available in *The Hellenistic Philosophers*, by A. A. Long and D. N. Sedley (Cambridge, 1987; volume 1 contains English translations of the Greek and Latin texts in volume 2).

There are many histories which cover all or part of this early development of philosophy; one especially worth recommending is the *History of Ancient Philosophy* by Giovanni Reale (translated by John R. Catan), consisting of four volumes: *From the Origins to Socrates* (Albany, 1987); *Plato and Aristotle* (Albany, 1990); *The Systems of the Hellenistic Age* (Albany, 1985); *The Schools of the Imperial Age* (Albany, 1990). The preface of the first volume contains a brief but excellent discussion of the relationship between classical philosophy and the "crisis"of modern philosophy; one of the many virtues of the second volume is its sophisticated understanding of the relationship between Plato's and Aristotle's thought. For an introduction to Plato and Aristotle with a keen sense of their continuing social importance, one can do no better than Eric Voegelin, *Order and History, Vol. 3: Plato and Aristotle* (Baton Rouge, LA, 1957).

⅋

AMONG MEDIEVAL WRITERS, the two most obviously worth mentioning are **Augustine of Hippo** (354–430) and **Thomas Aquinas** (1225–1274).

Philosophy plays a major role in Augustine's intellectual development and conversion to Christianity, and Augustine's own story of that development, the *Confessions*, is perhaps the best introduction to Augustine's thought; it is available in many translations. After *Confessions*, students should turn to Augustine's greatest work, *The City of God*. Other works of particular philosophical interest include *De Magistro* ("*On the Teacher*"), *Contra Academicos* ("*Against the Skeptics*"), and *De Natura Boni* ("*On the Nature of the Good*"). A good introduction to the life and thought of Augustine is Vernon J. Bourke, *Augustine's Quest of Wisdom* (Milwaukee, 1945).

Even the least complex works of Aquinas require a

great deal of preparation to appreciate, and his grand masterpieces really must be approached with the help of a careful teacher. Nonetheless, the beginning student can benefit from reading the *Summa Contra Gentiles*. A recent and sensitive guide to this text is Thomas Hibbs, *Dialectic and Narrative in Aquinas: An Interpretation of the Summa Contra Gentiles* (Notre Dame, IN, 1995).

One may also do well to turn to one of the many compilations of texts available. Anton C. Pegis's *Introduction to Saint Thomas Aquinas* (New York, 1945), contains mostly selections from the *Summa Theologiae*; Ralph McInerny's *Thomas Aquinas: Selected Writings* (New York, 1998), includes selections from a wider range of Thomas's writings, with helpful short introductions to each section.

It is possible to name several valuable secondary sources on Aquinas, but no single volume better conveys the spirit and import of Aquinas's thought than G. K. Chesterton's classic book, *St. Thomas Aquinas* (New York, 1933). Other useful treatments of Aquinas include: F. C. Copleston, *Aquinas* (Baltimore, 1955); Etienne Gilson, *The Philosophy of St. Thomas Aquinas* (New

York, 1956); Vernon J. Bourke, *Aquinas' Search for Wisdom* (Milwaukee, 1965); Jacques Maritain, *St. Thomas Aquinas* (New York, 1964); and Ralph McInerny, *St. Thomas Aquinas* (Notre Dame, IN, 1977). McInerny has also written a book designed especially for a beginning student of Aquinas: *A First Glance at St. Thomas Aquinas: A Handbook for Peeping Thomists* (Notre Dame, IN, 1990). Another useful book is Frederick Wilhelmsen, *Man's Knowledge of Reality: An Introduction to Thomistic Epistemology* (Englewood Cliffs, NJ, 1956).

From Augustine and Aquinas, the list of important medieval philosophers must be extended to include at least **Boethius**, **Anselm**, **Duns Scotus**, and **William Ockham**. Boethius (480–524) played an important role as a commentator on Aristotle's logical treatises, but the beginning student is more likely to benefit from a careful reading of a very different sort of work, composed in exile before execution, *The Consolation of Philosophy*; from this great work much can be learned about the classical understanding of philosophy. Of Anselm (1033–1109) one should read *Proslogion*, with its famous discussions of the relationships between faith and reason and proofs for the existence of God. For the beginning student, Scotus (1270–1308) and Ockham (or Occam, 1280–1349) will be important primarily as presenting alternatives to Aquinas; though both Scotus and Ockham still considered themselves a part of an Aristotelian tradition, their views represent a radical break with the achievement of Aquinas. Widely available are the not entirely reliable translations of selections: Allan Wolter, *Duns Scotus: Philosophical Writings* (London, 1962); and Philotheus Boehner, *William of Ockham: Philosophical Writings* (London, 1955).

These names are only representative, and cannot do justice to the diversely populated field of medieval thinkers. Not to be ignored are the Neoplatonist figures of the early middle ages; the essays collected in *The Cambridge History of Later Greek and Early Medieval Philosophy*, edited by A. H. Armstrong (Cambridge, 1967), provide helpful background. For an introduction to perhaps the best representative of Neoplatonic thought, **Plotinus** (204–270), one can turn to Emile Brehier, *The Philosophy of Plotinus* (Chicago, 1958). For selections of medieval texts from a wide range of medieval thinkers, including some of the influential **Jewish** and **Arabic thinkers**, there are several edited collections commonly used in introductory philosophy courses: Arthur Hyman and James J. Walsh, *Philosophy in the Middle Ages* (Indianapolis, 1967; second edition, 1973); John F. Wippel and Allan B. Wolter, *Medieval Philosophy: From St. Augustine to Nicholas of Cusa* (New York, 1969); Herman Shapiro, *Medieval Philosophy: Selected Readings from Augustine to Buridan* (New York, 1964). Older than these, but still valuable for its introductory notes, is Richard McKeon, *Selections from Medieval Philosophers (Vol. 1: Augustine to Albert the Great*, New York, 1929; *Vol. 2: Roger Bacon to William of Ockham*, New York, 1930).

For introductory histories of medieval philosophy, the following are highly recommended as worthwhile narratives: Josef Pieper, *Scholasticism: Personalities and Problems of Medieval Philosophy* (New York, 1960); Etienne Gilson, *The Spirit of Medieval Philosophy* (New York, 1940); Gerald Walsh, *Medieval Humanism* (New York, 1942); David Knowles, *The Evolution of Medieval Thought* (Baltimore, 1962; second edition, 1986); and Frederick C. Copleston, *A History of Medieval Philoso-*

phy (New York, 1972). Maurice de Wulf focuses on Thomas Aquinas as a model in his influential introduction to medieval thought, *Medieval Philosophy* (Cambridge, 1922). John Marenbon's *Later Medieval Philosophy (1150–1350)* (London, 1987; revised, 1994) includes helpful background information about the influences on and conventions of late medieval education. A useful introductory guide to both ancient and medieval thought is James N. Jordan, *Western Philosophy: From Antiquity to the Middle Ages* (New York, 1987).

❦

MODERN PHILOSOPHY IS SAID to begin—and so the tradition of classical philosophy is often said to end—with **René Descartes** (1596–1650). To get a sense of Descartes's approach to philosophy, one should read first the *Meditations on First Philosophy* (1641), which can be supplemented with *Discourse on the Method* (1637); again, as with all of the classic texts mentioned here, these works are available in numerous editions. As a general treatment of Descartes's thought, Anthony Kenny, *Descartes: A Study of His Philosophy* (New York,

1968) is fairly accessible. Criticism of Descartes's approach to philosophy and its legacy for the history of philosophy, expressed in this guide, is presented at greater length in Etienne Gilson, *The Unity of Philosophical Experience* (New York, 1937). Also valuable is Jacque Maritain, *The Dream of Descartes* (New York, 1944), especially the final chapter, "The Cartesian Heritage."

What this guide refers to as "the epistemological turn" in the history of philosophy—the preoccupation with "the problem of knowledge" precipitated by Descartes's skeptical arguments—is manifested most obviously in the classic works of **John Locke** (1632–1704), **George Berkeley** (1685–1753), and **David Hume** (1711–1776): Locke's *Essay Concerning Human Understanding* (1689), Berkeley's *Principles of Human Knowledge* (1710), and Hume's *Enquiry Concerning the Human Understanding* (1748). The student of intellectual history who wants to appreciate the legacy of Descartes must become familiar with these works and with the next major figure in the history of ideas, **Immanuel Kant** (1724–1804). Among the most readable of Kant's notoriously difficult prose is *Prolegomena to Any Future Metaphysics* (1783) and

Foundations of (alternatively *Groundwork for*) *the Metaphysics of Morals* (1785). His most important work is *Critique of Pure Reason* (1781), and the translation by Norman Kemp Smith (London, 1934) is still the standard.

For the whole range of Kant's thought, Roger Scruton, *Kant* (Oxford, 1982) is a good general introduction. Richard Schacht's, *Classical Modern Philosophers: Descartes to Kant* (London, 1984) and Lewis White Beck's, *Early German Philosophy: Kant and His Predecessors* (Cambridge, MA, 1969) are helpful guides to this period of early modern philosophy. To understand all of these philosophers, one must have a general sense of what is still referred to as the European "Enlightenment," for which the student can turn to Robert Anchor, *The Enlightenment Tradition* (New York, 1967). Paul Hazard's, *The European Mind (1680–1715)* (London, 1953), is a classic and spirited discussion of a short but determinative period of the Enlightenment, and Thomas P. Neill's, *Makers of the Modern Mind* (Milwaukee, 1949) includes chapters on Descartes, Locke, and Kant, among others.

The next great name to mention in modern philosophy is **G. W. F. Hegel** (1770–1831). Those who dare to tackle Hegel may find some help from Charles Taylor, *Hegel* (Oxford, 1975); some sense of Hegel's most important work, *Phenomenology of Spirit* (1807), is made by Robert Solomon, *In the Spirit of Hegel* (Oxford, 1983).

Friedrich Nietzsche (1844–1900) is often understood as the culmination, or *reductio ad absurdum*, of modern philosophy, and after reading early modern philosophy it is difficult not to appreciate the spirit behind his essay *On the Use and Abuse of History* (1847; alternatively titled *On the Advantage and Disadvantage of History for Life* in the edition by Hackett). Students who want to get a better sense of his ethical nihilism should proceed to *Beyond Good and Evil* (1887) and *The Genealogy of Morals* (1887), most commonly found in the translations by Walter Kaufmann.

Kaufmann has also written a helpful book about Nietzsche's thought: *Nietzsche: Philosopher, Psychologist, Antichrist* (Princeton, NJ, 1950; fourth edition, 1974). For critical but persuasive presentations of the spirit and significance of Nietzsche and German thought generally, it is easy to recommend the essays of Erich Heller, collected in *The Disinherited Mind* (New York, 1975) and *The Importance of Nietzsche* (Chicago, 1988).

Another landmark in the lanscape of modern philosophy is **Martin Heidegger** (1889–1976). His great work *Being and Time* (1927) is available in two translations—the longtime standard translation by John Macquarrie and Eduard Robinson (New York, 1962) is now rivalled by the newer one by Joan Stambaugh (Albany, NY, 1996).

Ludwig Wittgenstein (1889–1951) is often treated as two different people because of the difference between his early work—*Tractatus Logico-philosophicus* (1921)—and his later work—*Philosophical Investigations* (1953). Anthony Kenny's, *Wittgenstein* (Harmondsworth, UK, 1983) provides an introduction to both. Wittgenstein was influenced by the important logician **Gottlob Frege** (1848–1925), an excellent introduction to whom can be found in the classic by G. E. M. Anscombe and P. T. Geach, *Three Philosophers* (Ithaca, NY, 1961), which also includes valuable essays on Aristotle and Aquinas. Claire

Ortiz Hill offers an interpretation of the legacy of these and other thinkers in *Rethinking Identity and Metaphysics: On the Foundations of Analytic Philosophy* (New Haven, CT, 1997).

This guide makes reference to two other influential twentieth century books: A. J. Ayer, *Language, Truth and Logic* (1936; second edition, 1946) and G. E. Moore, *Principia Ethica* (New York, 1903). For a brief introduction to the significance of these works in the development of moral philosophy, see James Rachels, "Introduction: Moral Philosophy in the Twentieth Century," in *Twentieth Century Ethical Theory*, edited by Steven M. Cahn and Joram G. Haber (Englewood Cliffs, NJ, 1995). For a general introduction to the history of ethics, see Alasdair MacIntyre, *A Short History of Ethics* (New York, 1966; second edition, 1998). Alasdair MacIntyre's *After Virtue* (Notre Dame, IN, 1981; second edition, 1984) offers a critique of the Enlightenment legacy in ethics that is justly famous and widely influential. A criticism of what MacIntyre calls "emotivism" can also be found in C. S. Lewis, *The Abolition of Man* (London, 1944), an excellent introduction to ethics and to philosophy generally.

For essays on the major figures in the history of political thought, see Leo Strauss and Joseph Crospey, editors, *History of Political Philosophy* (Chicago, 1963; third edition, 1987); the third edition contains a valuable epilogue on Leo Strauss and his discernment of and response to "the crisis of modernity." For a criticism of the tradition of modern liberal political theory, recently exemplified most prominently by John Rawls in *A Theory of Justice* (Cambridge, MA, 1971), see George Parkin Grant, *English Speaking Justice* (Sackville, NB, Canada, 1974; Notre Dame, 1985), which argues persuasively for the continuing importance of classical philosophy. The reciprocal influences of modern philosophy and modern politics are treated in Harry Redner, *Malign Masters: Gentile, Heidegger, Lukács, Wittgenstein: Philosophy and Politics in the Twentieth Century* (New York, 1997).

For general histories of modern philosophy, see Roger Scruton, *A Short History of Modern Philosophy: From Descartes to Wittgenstein* (London, 1995; revision of *From Descartes to Wittgenstein*, 1981). More recent thought is treated in John Passmore, *A Hundred Years of Philosophy*

(London, 1957; revised, New York, 1966), in Passmore's 1985 supplement, *Recent Philosophers,* and in Roger Scruton, *Modern Philosophy: An Introduction and Survey* (London, 1994).

⁂

FOR RECENT SECONDARY literature on figures spanning the history of philosophy, with up-to-date bibliographic references and a sense of the state of scholarship on particular authors, one can turn to the many volumes in the growing Cambridge Companions series, whose titles each begin with *A Cambridge Companion to [philosopher's name].* For an overview of the history of philosophy, one can turn to Paul J. Glenn, *The History of Philosophy* (St. Louis, 1954); Julián Marias, *History of Philosophy* (New York, 1967); or Anthony Kenny, *A Brief History of Western Philosophy* (Oxford, 1998). However, for a more thorough history, Frederick C. Copleston's magisterial *A History of Philosophy,* nine volumes (1944–1975), is unsurpassed and still in print.

There are many books which are not properly books of or about philosophy which can nevertheless help introduce students to philosophy. An exciting work which stimulates the philosophical intellect is Richard Weaver, *Ideas Have Consequences* (Chicago, 1948). Allan Bloom's highly controversial *The Closing of the American Mind* (New York, 1987) contains among other things some provocative arguments about the philosophical origins of modernity (see especially parts II and III). And last but hardly least, the role of philosophy in education is persuasively articulated in a book that should be read by all students: John Henry Newman's *The Idea of a University* (1852).

EMBARKING ON A LIFELONG PURSUIT OF KNOWLEDGE?

*Take Advantage of These New Resources
& a New Website*

❦

The ISI Guides to the Major Disciplines are part of the Intercollegiate Studies Institute's (ISI) **Student Self-Reliance Project**, an integrated, sequential program of educational supplements designed to guide students in making key decisions that will enable them to acquire an appreciation of the accomplishments of Western civilization.

Developed with fifteen months of detailed advice from college professors and students, these resources provide advice in course selection and guidance in actual coursework. The project elements can be used independently by students to navigate the existing university curriculum in a way that deepens their understanding of our Western intellectual heritage. As indicated below, the Project's integrated components will answer key questions at each stage of a student's education.

What are the strengths and weaknesses of the most selective schools?
Choosing the Right College directs prospective college students to the best and worst that top American colleges have to offer.

What is the essence of a liberal arts education?
A Student's Guide to Liberal Learning introduces students to the vital connection between liberal education and political liberty.

What core courses should every student take?
A Student's Guide to the Core Curriculum instructs students in building their own core curricula, utilizing electives available at virtually every university, and discusses how to identify and overcome contemporary political biases in those courses.

How can students learn from the best minds in their major fields of study?
Student Guides to the Major Disciplines introduce students to overlooked and misrepresented classics, facilitating work within their majors. Guides currently available assess the fields of literature, philosophy, U.S. history, economics, political philosophy, classics, psychology, general history, liberal learning, the core curriculum, and American political thought.

Which great modern thinkers are neglected?
The Library of Modern Thinkers will introduce students to great minds who have contributed to the literature of the West but are nevertheless neglected or denigrated in today's classroom. Figures in this series include Robert Nisbet, Eric Voegelin, Wilhelm Röpke, Ludwig von Mises, Michael Oakeshott, Andrew Nelson Lytle, Bertrand de Jouvenal, and others.

Check out **www.collegeguide.org** for more information and to access unparalleled resources for making the most of your college experience.

ISI is a one-stop resource for serious students of all ages. Visit **www.isi.org** or call **1-800-526-7022** to add your name to the 50,000-plus ISI membership list of teachers, students, and professors.